G000065885

Dinner
IN FIVE

30 *low-carb* dinners

Up to 5 net carbs, 5 ingredients & 5 easy steps for every recipe

Vicky Ushakova and Rami Abramov

Table of Contents

Disclaimer

Tasteaholics, Inc. is not a medical company or organization. Our books provide information in respect to healthy eating, nutrition and recipes and are intended for informational purposes only. We are not nutritionists or doctors and the information in this book and our website is not meant to be given as medical advice. We are two people sharing our success strategies and resources and encouraging you to do further research to see if they'll work for you too. Before starting any diet, you should always consult with your physician to rule out any health issues that could arise. Safety first, results second. Do not disregard professional medical advice or delay in seeking it because of this book.

Photography: © Sea Wave/Bigstock.com, p. 4; Utima/Bigstock.com, p. 5; egal/Bigstock.com, p. 12; BelayaKaterina/Envato.com, p. 18; Nika111/Bigstock.com, p. 21; zmaris/Depositphotos.com, p. 21; kornienkoalex/Depositphotos.com, p. 21; scukrov/Depositphotos.com, p. 21; tashka2000/Bigstock.com, p. 22; ersler/Bigstock.com, p. 23; ivankmit/Envato.com, p. 24; janstarstud/Bigstock.com, p. 26; dionisvera/Bigstock.com, p. 27; elenathewise/Bigstock.com, p. 30; Artem Merzlenko/Bigstock.com, p. 30; Natika/Bigstock.com, p. 32; indigolotos/Bigstock.com, p. 34; Natalia Zakharova/Bigstock.com, p. 36; JohanSwanepoel/Bigstock.com, p. 40; Madlen/Bigstock.com, p. 48; Eskymaks/Bigstock.com, p. 50; kozzi2/Depositphotos.com, p. 52; SvetlanaK/Bigstock.com, p. 54; sommai/Bigstock.com, p. 54; margouillat photo/Bigstock.com, p. 56; anphotos/Bigstock.com, p. 58; svry/Bigstock.com, p. 58; alexfiodorov/Bigstock.com, p. 60; jirkaejc/Bigstock.com, p. 62; Yastremska/Bigstock.com, p. 64; etorres69/Depositphotos.com, p. 64; Maria Komar/Bigstock.com, p. 66; lubastock/Bigstock.com, p. 68; Valentina R./Bigstock.com, p. 70; Gresei/Bigstock.com, p. 70; mazzzur/Depositphotos.com, p. 72; HandmadePictures/Bigstock.com, p. 74; exopixel/Bigstock.com, p. 74; Kovaleva Katerina/Bigstock.com, p. 76; klenova/Bigstock.com, p. 78; loflo/Bigstock.com, p. 78; pioneer111/Depositphotos.com, p. 80; lisovskaya/Bigstock.com, p. 82; Robyn Mackenzie/Bigstock.com, p. 86; lenka/Bigstock.com, p. 88; barbaradudzinska/Bigstock.com, p. 89.

About This Book

This book was designed as a guide to help you kick start your ketogenic diet so you can lose weight, become healthy and have high energy levels every day.

Inside this book, you'll find the basics of the ketogenic diet, useful tips and delicious dinner recipes.

Each recipe is only 5 grams of net carbs or fewer and can be made with just 5 ingredients! There's nothing better than that.

Eating low-carb doesn't require cutting out wholesome, nutritious foods or sacrificing taste — ever. We hand selected each ingredient to not only serve a delicious purpose but provide nutritious benefits.

Enjoy 30 delicious and easy low-carb dinner recipes including unconventional burgers, heavenly steaks, gourmet-style seafood, mouthwatering sauces and sides that'll keep you full and excited for tomorrow's dinner.

Let's get started!

Keto 101

What Is Keto?

The Ketogenic Diet

The ketogenic (or keto) diet is a low-carbohydrate, high-fat diet. Maintaining this diet is a great tool for weight loss. More importantly, according to an increasing number of studies, it reduces risk factors for diabetes, heart diseases, stroke, Alzheimer's, epilepsy, and more.[1-6]

On the keto diet, your body enters a metabolic state called ketosis. While in ketosis your body is using ketone bodies for energy instead of glucose. Ketone bodies are derived from fat and are a much more stable, steady source of energy than glucose, which is derived from carbohydrates.

Entering ketosis usually takes anywhere from 3 days to a week. Once you're in ketosis, you'll be using fat for energy, instead of carbs. This includes the fat you eat and stored body fat.

While eating low-carb, you'll lose weight easier, feel satiated longer and enjoy consistent energy levels throughout your day.

Testing for Ketosis

You can test yourself to see whether you've entered ketosis just a few days after you've begun the keto diet! Use a *ketone urine test strip* and it will tell you the level of ketone bodies in your urine. If the concentration is high enough and the test strip shows any hue of purple, you've successfully entered ketosis!

The strips take only a few seconds to show results and are the fastest and most affordable way to check whether you're in ketosis.

Visit tasteaholics.com/strips and get a bottle of 100 test strips.

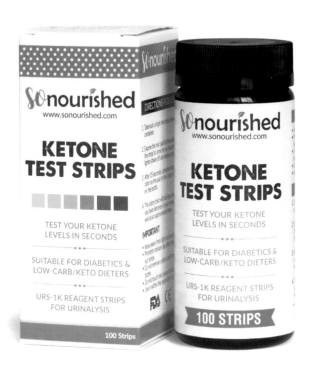

The Truth About Fat

You may be thinking, "but eating a lot of fat is bad!" The truth is, dozens of studies and meta studies with over 900,000 subjects have arrived at similar conclusions: eating saturated and monounsaturated fats have no effects on heart disease risks.[7,8]

Most fats are good and are essential to our health. Fats (fatty acids) and protein (amino acids) are essential for survival.

> There is no such thing as an essential carbohydrate.

Fats are the most efficient form of energy and each gram contains more than double the energy in a gram of protein or carbohydrates (more on that later).

The keto diet promotes eating fresh, whole foods like meat, fish, veggies, and healthy fats and oils as well as greatly reducing processed and chemically treated foods the Standard American Diet (SAD) has so long encouraged.

It's a diet that you can sustain long-term and enjoy. What's not to enjoy about bacon and eggs in the morning?

9

Calories & Macro-nutrients

How Calories Work

A calorie is a unit of energy. When something contains 100 calories, it describes how much energy your body could get from consuming it. Calorie consumption dictates weight gain/loss.

If you burn an average of 1,800 calories and eat 2,000 calories per day, you will gain weight.

If you do light exercise that burns an extra 300 calories per day, you'll burn 2,100 calories per day, putting you at a deficit of 100 calories. Simply by eating at a deficit, you will lose weight because your body will tap into stored resources for the remaining energy it needs.

That being said, it's important to get the right balance of macronutrients every day so your body has the energy it needs.

tasteaholics.com/calculator

What Are Macronutrients?

Macronutrients (macros) are molecules that our bodies use to create energy for themselves – primarily fat, protein and carbs. They are found in all food and are measured in grams (g) on nutrition labels.

- **Fat** provides 9 calories per gram
- **Protein** provides 4 calories per gram
- **Carbs** provide 4 calories per gram

Learn more at tasteaholics.com/macros.

Net Carbs

Most low-carb recipes write net carbs when displaying their macros. Net carbs are total carbs minus dietary fiber and sugar alcohols. Our bodies can't break them down into glucose so they don't count toward your total carb count.

Note: *Dietary fiber can be listed as soluble or insoluble.*

How Much Should You Eat?

On a keto diet, about 65 to 75 percent of the calories you consume daily should come from fat. About 20 to 30 percent should come from protein. The remaining 5 percent or so should come from carbohydrates.

Use our keto calculator to figure out exactly how many calories and macros you should be eating every day!

It will ask for basic information including your weight, activity levels and goals and instantly provide you with the total calories and grams of fat, protein and carbs that you should be eating each day.

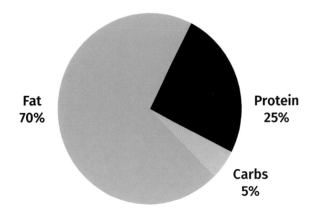

Note: *The calculator should be used as a general guideline. The results are based on your inputs and variables such as body fat percentage and basal metabolic rate are difficult to estimate correctly.*

A Nutritional Revolution

Carbs: What Exactly Are They?

Carbohydrates (carbs) are found in things like starches, grains and foods high in sugar. This includes, but isn't limited to, bread, flour, rice, pasta, beans, potatoes, sugar, syrup, cereals, fruits, bagels and soda.

Carbs are broken down into glucose (a type of sugar) in our bodies for energy. Eating any kinds of carbs spikes blood sugar levels. The spike may happen faster or slower depending on the type of carb (based on the glycemic index), but the spike will still happen.

Blood sugar spikes cause strong insulin releases to combat the spikes. Constant insulin releases result in fat storage and insulin resistance. After many years, this cycle can lead to prediabetes, metabolic syndrome and even type 2 diabetes.[9]

In a world full of sugar, cereal, pasta, burgers, French fries and large sodas, you can see how carbs can easily be overconsumed.

> "Almost 1 in 10 adults in the U.S.
> have type 2 diabetes,
> nearly 4 times more than 30 years ago."

Where We Are Today

According to the 2014 report by the Centers for Disease Control and Prevention (CDC), more than 1 in 3 adults in the U.S. (86 million people) have prediabetes, a condition in which blood glucose is always high and commonly leads to type 2 diabetes and many other medical problems.[10]

Today, almost 1 in 10 people in the U.S. have type 2 diabetes compared to almost 1 in 40 in 1980.

Fat has been blamed as the bad guy and carbohydrates have been considered crucial and healthy. Companies have been creating low-fat and fat-free, chemical-laden alternatives of nearly every type of food in existence, yet diabetes and heart disease rates are still increasing.

Fat Is Making a Comeback

Hundreds of studies have been conducted in the past ten years which have been corroborating the same data: that eating healthy fats is not detrimental to health and is, in fact, more beneficial than eating a diet high in carbohydrates.

We're starting to understand that carbs in large quantities are much more harmful than previously thought, while most fats are healthy and essential.

The nutritional landscape is changing. Low-carb and similar dietary groups are growing and a nutritional revolution is beginning. We are beginning to realize the detrimental effects of our relationship with excess sugar and carbs.

The Basics: Benefits of Going Keto

Long-Term Benefits

Studies consistently show that those who eat a low-carb, high-fat diet rather than a high-carb, low-fat diet:

- Lose more weight and body fat[11-17]

- Have better levels of good cholesterol (HDL and large LDL)[18,19]

- Have reduced blood sugar and insulin resistance (commonly reversing prediabetes and type 2 diabetes)[20,21]

- Experience a decrease in appetite[22]

- Have reduced triglyceride levels (fat molecules in the blood that cause heart disease)[19,23]

- Have significant reductions in blood pressure, leading to a reduction in heart disease and stroke[24]

> Eating keto/low-carb
> helps you lose more weight
> than eating low-fat.

Day-To-Day Benefits

The keto diet doesn't only provide long-term benefits! When you're on keto, you can expect to:

- Lose body fat
- Have stable energy levels during the day
- Stay satiated after meals longer, with less snacking and overeating

Longer satiation and consistent energy levels are due to the majority of calories coming from fat, which is slower to digest and calorically denser.

Eating low-carb also eliminates blood glucose spikes and crashes. You won't have sudden blood sugar drops leaving you feeling weak and disoriented.

Entering Ketosis

The keto diet's main goal is to keep you in nutritional ketosis all the time. If you're just getting started with your keto diet, you should eat up to 25 grams of carbs per day.

Once you're in ketosis for long enough (about 4 to 8 weeks), you become keto-adapted, or fat-adapted. This is when your glycogen stores in muscles and liver are depleted, you carry less water weight, muscle endurance increases and your overall energy levels are higher.

Once keto-adapted, you can usually eat ≈50 grams of net carbs a day to maintain ketosis.

Type 1 Diabetes & Ketoacidosis

If you have type 1 diabetes, consult with your doctor before starting a keto diet. Diabetic ketoacidosis (DKA) is a dangerous condition that can occur if you have type 1 diabetes due to a shortage of insulin.

Steering Clear of the Keto Flu

What Is the Keto Flu?

The keto flu happens commonly to keto dieters due to low levels of sodium and electrolytes and has flu-like symptoms including:

- Fatigue
- Headaches
- Cough
- Sniffles
- Irritability
- Nausea

It's important to note that this isn't the real flu! It's called keto flu due to similar symptoms but it is not at all contagious and doesn't actually involve a virus.

Why Does It Happen?

The main cause of keto flu is your body lacking electrolytes, especially sodium. When starting keto, you cut out lots of processed foods and eat more whole, natural foods. Although this is great, it causes a sudden drop in sodium intake.

> **The keto flu can be avoided by consuming enough electrolytes, especially sodium.**

In addition, reducing carbs reduces insulin levels, which reduces sodium stored by kidneys.[25]

Between your reduced sodium intake and stored sodium flushed by your kidneys, you end up being low on sodium and other electrolytes.

Ending the Keto Flu

The best way to avoid or end the keto flu is to add more sodium and electrolytes to your diet. Here are the most effective (and tasty) ways to get more sodium:

- Adding more salt to your food
- Drinking soup broth
- Eating plenty of salty foods like bacon and pickled vegetables

Try to eat more sodium as you start the keto diet to prevent the keto flu entirely. If you do catch it, just remember that it'll go away quickly and you'll emerge a fat-burning machine!

Note: *For more information about the keto flu, read our full guide at* tasteaholics.com/keto-flu.

Starting Keto

Part 1 — Out with the Old

Having tempting, unhealthy foods in your home is one of the biggest reasons for failure when starting any diet.

To maximize your chances of success, you need to remove as many triggers as you can. This crucial step will help prevent moments of weakness from ruining all your hard work.

If you aren't living alone, make sure to discuss with your family or housemates before throwing anything out. If some items are simply not yours to throw out, try to compromise and agree on a special location so you can keep them out of sight and out of mind.

Once your home is free of temptation, eating low-carb is far less difficult and success is that much easier.

Starches and Grains

Get rid of all cereal, pasta, bread, rice, potatoes, corn, oats, quinoa, flour, bagels, rolls, croissants and wraps.

All Sugary Things

Throw away and forget all refined sugar, fruit juices, desserts, fountain drinks, milk chocolate, pastries, candy bars, etc.

Legumes

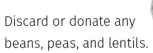

Discard or donate any beans, peas, and lentils.

Vegetable & Seed Oils

Stop using any vegetable oils and seed oils like sunflower, safflower, soybean, canola, corn and grapeseed oil. Get rid of trans fats like margarine.

Read Nutrition Labels

Check the nutrition labels on all your products to see if they're high in carbs. There are hidden carbs in the unlikeliest of places (like ketchup and canned soups). Try to avoid buying products with dozens of incomprehensible ingredients. Less is usually healthier.

For example:

> Deli ham can have 2 or 3 grams of sugar per slice as well as many added preservatives and nitrites!

Always check the serving sizes against the carb counts. Manufacturers can sometimes recommend inconceivably small serving sizes to seemingly reduce calorie and carb numbers.

At first glance, something may be low in carbs, but a quick comparison to the serving size can reveal the product is mostly sugar. Be diligent!

Nutrition Facts

Serving Size 1 Cup (53g/1.9 oz.)
Servings Per Container About 8

Amount Per Serving		
Calories 190	Calories from Fat 25	
		% Daily Value*
Total Fat 3g		5%
Saturated Fat 0g		0%
Trans Fat 0g		
Cholesterol 0mg		0%
Sodium 100mg		4%
Potassium 300mg		9%
Total Carbohydrate 37g		12%
Dietary Fiber 8g		32%
Soluble Fiber		
Insoluble Fibe		
Sugars 13g		
Protein 9g		14%
Vitamin A 0%		C 0%
Calcium 4%		10%

Part 2 – In with the New!

Now that you've cleaned out everything you don't need, it's time to restock your pantry and fridge with delicious and wholesome, keto-friendly foods that will help you lose weight, become healthier, and feel amazing!

General Products to Have

With these basics in your home, you'll always be ready to make healthy, keto-friendly meals.

- Lots of water, coffee, and unsweetened tea
- Stevia and erythritol (sweeteners)
- Condiments like mayonnaise, mustard, pesto, and sriracha
- Broths (beef, chicken, bone)
- Pickles and other fermented foods
- Seeds and nuts (chia seeds, flaxseeds, pecans, almonds, walnuts, macadamias, etc.)

Meat, Fish & Eggs

Just about every type of fresh meat and fish is good for keto including beef, chicken, lamb, pork, salmon, tuna, etc. Eat grass-fed and/or organic meat and wild-caught fish whenever possible.

Eat as many eggs as you like, preferably organic from free-range chickens.

Vegetables

Eat plenty of non-starchy veggies including asparagus, mushrooms, broccoli, cucumber, lettuce, onions, peppers, cauliflower, tomatoes, garlic, Brussels sprouts and zucchini.

Dairy

You can eat full-fat dairy like sour cream, heavy (whipping) cream, butter, cheeses and unsweetened yogurt.

Although not dairy, unsweetened almond milk and coconut milk are both good milk substitutes.

Stay away from regular milk, skim milk and sweetened yogurts because they contain a lot of sugar. Avoid all fat-free and low-fat dairy products.

Oils and Fats

Olive oil, avocado oil, butter and bacon fat are great for cooking and consuming. Avocado oil is best for searing due to its very high smoke point (520°F).

Fruits

Berries like strawberries, blueberries, raspberries, etc. are allowed in small amounts. Avocados are great because they're low-carb and very high in fat!

Recipes

Notes

- We use large eggs in all our recipes. If yours are a different size, know that this will affect the nutrition slightly and even perhaps the end results.

- The low-carb protein powder we use is *Isopure* Vanilla and *Isopure* Chocolate.

- Almond milk and coconut milk is always the unsweetened variety.

- The mozzarella cheese in each recipe is a low-moisture, part-skim, shredded mozzarella cheese; not fresh mozzarella.

- Most recipes make 2 servings unless otherwise stated. The nutrition facts listed are per 1 serving.

- If you're not a fan of spicy foods, feel free to leave out ingredients like jalapeño peppers, hot sauce, red pepper flakes, etc.

- The marinara sauce we use in all our recipes is of the brand *Rao's Homemade Sauces*. They are a low-sugar or no sugar added tomato sauce maker which can be found in many supermarkets. You can also choose to make your own from scratch or use any low-sugar tomato sauce you have on hand.

- A food scale is a must if you're counting calories and macros. Many of our ingredients are listed by weight to provide accurate nutritional data.

Low-Carb Friendly Seasonings

The following herbs and spices may be used in any of our recipes should you wish to add them.

They are all low-carb though we suggest limiting them to under a tablespoon to stay within your daily goals. It's more than enough to add their delicious flavors to your dishes without putting you over your carb limit!

- ☐ Salt
- ☐ Pepper
- ☐ Paprika
- ☐ Cayenne
- ☐ Thyme
- ☐ Basil
- ☐ Oregano
- ☐ Parsley
- ☐ Rosemary
- ☐ Tarragon
- ☐ Sage
- ☐ Cumin
- ☐ Red pepper flakes
- ☐ Sesame seeds

Soy Sauce Ginger Pork

Asian inspired, sweet & salty pork over some basic, but delicious green beans. Dinner couldn't be simpler!

Nutrition

335 calories per serving | Makes 2 servings

20 grams of fat

37 grams of protein

5 grams of net carbs

Ingredients

- 2 6-oz. pork loin chops
- 2 tbsp. sesame seed oil
- ¼ cup soy sauce
- 1 inch ginger, minced
- 1 cup green beans

Instructions

1. Heat up a pan with sesame seed oil. Cook ginger until fragrant, about 3–5 minutes.
2. Add pork loin to the pan and cook for about 8 minutes on each side. In the last 3 minutes, add soy sauce. Spoon the soy sauce to coat the pork well while cooking.
3. Cook green beans in another pan on high heat until slightly browned.
4. Slice the pork chops and serve over a bed of green beans. Add an extra drizzle of soy sauce for even more flavor!

Cheesy Meatballs Parm

Meatballs are a simple, low-carb dinner staple that are popular with kids and adults alike!

Nutrition

575 calories per serving | Makes 2 servings

- 35 grams of fat
- 52 grams of protein
- 4 grams of net carbs

🕐 **Prep Time: 10 mins | Cook Time: 15 mins**

Ingredients

- 1 lb. ground beef
- 1 large egg, beaten
- ¼ cup Parmesan cheese
- ½ cup marinara sauce
- 200 grams zucchini

Instructions

1. Combine beef, egg and Parmesan plus seasonings of your choice. Roll into 1" balls.
2. Pan sear meatballs on all sides on high heat. Lower flame, add marinara sauce and cook covered for 10 minutes.
3. Spiralize the zucchini into zoodles and cook them in a lightly oiled pan for no more than 2 minutes, tossing continuously.
4. Add meatballs to a bed of zoodles and enjoy!

Avocado Lime Salmon

One of our favorite salmon recipes is smothered in a zesty avocado lime sauce atop delicate riced cauliflower!

Nutrition

420 calories per serving | Makes 2 servings

- 27 grams of fat
- 37 grams of protein
- 5 grams of net carbs

Ingredients

- 2 6-oz. salmon fillets
- 1 medium avocado
- ½ lime, juiced
- 2 tbsp. red onion
- 100 grams cauliflower florets

Instructions

1. Rice the cauliflower florets in a food processor and cook them in an oiled pan on low heat, covered, for 8 minutes.
2. Blend the avocado, juice of ½ lime, salt & pepper until creamy and smooth. Set aside.
3. Heat a skillet on medium heat with some avocado or coconut oil and cook salmon for about 4–5 minutes on each side.
4. Serve with cauliflower rice and garnish with the avocado sauce and some diced red onion.

Lemon Rosemary Chicken

Grilled & seasoned simply, this flavorful chicken breast recipe is easy to make and pairs well with cauliflower mashed potatoes.

Nutrition

400 calories per serving | Makes 2 servings

26 grams of fat

39 grams of protein

3 grams of net carbs

🕐 **Prep Time: 1 hour | Cook Time: 25 mins**

Ingredients

- 2 8-oz. chicken breasts
- ½ lemon
- 1 sprig fresh rosemary
- ½ head cauliflower, broken into florets
- 4 tbsp. unsalted butter, melted

Instructions

1. Pound the chicken breasts until ½ inch thick.
2. Marinade them for an hour in the juice of ½ a lemon, salt, pepper and rosemary needles.
3. Steam the cauliflower florets, then blend them with butter. Season with salt and pepper.
4. Grill or fry the chicken breasts until cooked, about 7 minutes on each side.
5. Serve the chicken breast on a bed of the cauliflower mashed potatoes and enjoy!

Chicken Parmesan

An Italian classic turned low-carb with the help of one special ingredient! Make this recipe for dinner and enjoy juicy, crispy chicken breasts!

Nutrition

425 calories per serving | Makes 2 servings

| 23 grams of fat
| 52 grams of protein
| 2 grams of net carbs

Ingredients

- 2 6-oz. chicken breasts
- 1 large egg, beaten
- ¼ cup Parmesan cheese
- 2 oz. pork rinds
- ½ cup marinara sauce

Instructions

1. Pulse the pork rinds and Parmesan in a food processor until they resemble bread crumbs.
2. Coat the chicken breasts in the beaten egg then the low-carb breading, pressing firmly.
3. Bake the breaded chicken breasts in a 375°F oven for 30 minutes.
4. Add marinara sauce to each chicken breast 5 minutes before they're done cooking.
5. Serve with a sprinkle of more Parmesan cheese and dried spices of your choice (see page 27).

Sweet Pork Tenderloin

Craving something sweet? Some apple will do the trick — layered over pork tenderloin, it provides the perfect sweet pairing.

Nutrition

420 calories per serving | Makes 2 servings

28 grams of fat

37 grams of protein

5 grams of net carbs

Ingredients

- 2 6-oz. pork loin chops
- 40 grams sliced apple
- 2-4 sprigs rosemary
- 4 tbsp. unsalted butter
- 200 grams cauliflower

Instructions

1. Season pork loins with salt and pepper. Sear them on both sides in a well-oiled pan on high heat.
2. Lower the flame and add sliced apple and a sprig of rosemary to the top of the pork loins. Cover and cook for about 8 minutes.
3. Steam the cauliflower florets, then blend them with butter. Season with salt and pepper.
4. Serve the pork loin chops with a fresh sprig of rosemary and alongside the cauliflower mashed potatoes.

Sloppy Joe

A family favorite, now low-carb and under 5 ingredients! Enjoy it all on its own or on Oopsie rolls.

Nutrition

640 calories per serving | Makes 2 servings

50 grams of fat

38 grams of protein

2 grams of net carbs

Ingredients

- 1 lb. ground beef
- ½ green bell pepper
- ½ cup marinara sauce
- 1 tbsp. Dijon mustard
- 1 tbsp. soy sauce

Instructions

1. Chop bell pepper and fry in an oiled pan on medium heat until softened.
2. Add the ground beef to the pan and break it up into small pieces using a wooden spoon.
3. Cook beef until brown, then add marinara, Dijon mustard and soy sauce. Season with salt and pepper to taste.
4. Continue to cook until the ground beef has cooked through and everything has thickened a bit.

Zesty Shrimp Skewers

Fun to make and more fun to eat! These zesty lemon skewers are full of flavor & pair nicely with our creamy avocado lime sauce.

Nutrition

440 calories per serving | Makes 2 servings

	33 grams of fat
	38 grams of protein
	3 grams of net carbs

🕐 **Prep Time: 10 mins | Cook Time: 8 mins**

Ingredients

- 16 oz. large shrimp, peeled
- 1 medium avocado
- 3 tbsp. mayonnaise
- 1 lime
- 2 cups frisée (or baby spinach)

Instructions

1. Defrost shrimp if necessary and thread them onto bamboo skewers.
2. Fry or grill the shrimp for about 3 minutes on each side or until fully pink.
3. Blend the avocado, mayonnaise, the juice of one lime and salt and pepper together in a small blender.
4. Serve the shrimp on a bed of frisée (or baby spinach) and drizzle them with the zesty avocado lime sauce.

Tip: *Moisten the bamboo skewers before threading to prevent them from catching fire.*

Extra Crispy Chicken Thighs

There's nothing like a crisp skin on a juicy chicken thigh. In this recipe, you'll broil chicken thighs with lemon and garlic!

Nutrition

635 calories per serving | Makes 2 servings

46 grams of fat

43 grams of protein

3 grams of net carbs

⏱ **Prep Time: 10 mins | Cook Time: 25 mins**

Ingredients

- 4 boneless chicken thighs
- ½ lemon
- 2 cloves garlic, sliced thinly
- 4 tbsp. unsalted butter
- 200 grams zucchini

Instructions

1. Season the chicken thighs with lemon juice, salt and pepper.
2. Arrange sliced garlic on top and set them onto a baking sheet lined with a cooling rack. Bake at 350°F for 25 minutes.
3. Slice zucchini and fry in olive oil until softened.
4. Add a tablespoon of butter onto each thigh and broil for 5 minutes.
5. Enjoy the chicken thighs with fried zucchini.

Pork Chops in Mushroom Sauce

A delicate yet robust, creamy mushroom sauce drizzled over pork chops for a very filling dinner!

Nutrition

790 calories per serving | Makes 2 servings

53 grams of fat

46 grams of protein

5 grams of net carbs

🕐 **Prep Time: 5 mins | Cook Time: 30 mins**

Ingredients

- ¼ white onion, diced
- 16 oz. white or brown mushrooms
- 2 tbsp. unsalted butter
- ½ cup heavy cream
- 2 8-oz. pork chops

Instructions

1. Start by sautéing the onion in an oiled pan until translucent.
2. Then add mushrooms and butter and cook until mushrooms have shrunk a bit. Add heavy cream and simmer sauce until it thickens, about 10 minutes.
3. In another pan, cook pork chops for 5–7 minutes on each side. Serve with the mushroom sauce.

47

Marinara Poached Cod

Delicate cod poached in a flavorful tomato sauce paired with green beans makes a great, light dinner!

Nutrition

390 calories per serving | Makes 2 servings

20 grams of fat

43 grams of protein

5 grams of net carbs

Ingredients

- 2 8-oz. cod fillets
- 2 tbsp. olive oil
- ½ cup marinara sauce
- 3 bay leaves
- 2 cups green beans

Instructions

1. Heat olive oil and marinara in a pan on medium heat. Add bay leaves, salt, pepper and a cup of water. Let it simmer for 5 minutes.
2. Lower the flame and add the cod fillets. Cover and cook for about 10 minutes, flipping once in between.
3. In another pan, sauté green beans in olive oil on medium-high heat for about 10 minutes.
4. Once the cod is cooked and opaque throughout, serve with the green beans and enjoy!

Buffalo Chicken Thighs

If you love buffalo wings, you'll love this recipe. These easy buffalo chicken thighs are a family favorite and are ultra low-carb.

Nutrition

745 calories per serving | Makes 2 servings

61 grams of fat	
45 grams of protein	
5 grams of net carbs	

Ingredients

- 4 boneless chicken thighs
- ¼ cup *Frank's Red Hot sauce*
- 2 tbsp. unsalted butter
- 2 cups green beans
- ¼ cup Bleu cheese dressing

Instructions

1. In an oven-safe pan on high heat, sear the thighs skin side down until golden. Flip and transfer to the oven for 20 minutes at 375°F.
2. Melt the butter and *Frank's Red Hot* sauce together on a very low flame, whisking well.
3. Coat the cooked chicken thighs in Frank's.
4. Fry the green beans in an oiled pan on medium-high heat until slightly browned.
5. Serve everything with Bleu cheese dressing.

Cheese Shell Tacos

Ultra low-carb tacos in mere minutes! Fill them up with your favorite fillings — ours are creamy and spicy, feel free to adjust.

Nutrition

580 calories per 2 tacos | Makes 4 tacos

- 43 grams of fat
- 39 grams of protein
- 5 grams of net carbs

🕐 **Prep Time: 10 mins | Cook Time: 30 mins**

Ingredients

- 1 cup shredded mozzarella cheese
- ½ lb. ground beef
- ½ cup sour cream
- ½ cup guacamole
- Sliced jalapeños (optional)

Instructions

1. Set a pan onto medium heat and melt ¼ cup of mozzarella cheese at a time until brown and caramelized.
2. Wedge a spatula underneath and drape the shell across a wooden spoon on a pot or between two glasses to cool into a taco shape.
3. Cook the ground beef and season with salt, pepper and any spices of your choice (see page 27).
4. Divide the ground beef equally into each taco shell, plus 2 tablespoons of sour cream, 2 tablespoons of guacamole & jalapeño slices (optional).

Mustard Lemon Salmon

Delicate salmon seared and cooked in a mustard lemon sauce to make a tangy and creamy dinner!

Nutrition

465 calories per serving | Makes 2 servings

32 grams of fat	
36 grams of protein	
1 gram of net carbs	

🕐 **Prep Time: 5 mins | Cook Time: 25 mins**

Ingredients

- 2 6-oz. salmon fillets
- ¼ cup heavy cream
- 1 tbsp. Dijon mustard
- 1 tbsp. lemon juice
- 100 grams cauliflower florets

Instructions

1. Rice the cauliflower in a food processor and cook in an oiled pan on low heat, covered, for 8 minutes, stirring ocassionally.
2. Heat another skillet on medium heat with olive oil and cook salmon for 3 minutes on each side. Then set aside.
3. Stir together heavy cream, mustard and lemon juice and add salmon back in for 5 minutes.
4. Serve everything on top of cauliflower rice.

Loaded Beef and Broccoli

Beef and broccoli makes dinner a breeze with common ingredients making it a go-to staple for your low-carb diet.

Nutrition

660 calories per serving | Makes 2 servings

41 grams of fat

60 grams of protein

5 grams of net carbs

🕐 **Prep Time: 5 mins | Cook Time: 25 mins**

Ingredients

- 100 grams broccoli
- 1 clove garlic
- 1 lb. ground beef
- 4 oz. shredded mozzarella
- 1 large egg

Instructions

1. Chop the broccoli and fry the florets in an oiled pan on high heat for 5-8 minutes.
2. Mince the garlic and add it in. Cook until fragrant and the broccoli softened.
3. Add the ground beef and break it up with a wooden spoon until cooked throughout.
4. Add the mozzarella cheese and the egg to mixture and stir well to incorporate.
5. Season with salt and pepper to taste and serve. Enjoy!

Soy Glazed Chicken

This Asian-inspired chicken marinade is absolutely delicious and will leave you craving more. Be sure to make plenty!

Nutrition

507 calories per serving | Makes 2 servings

- 38 grams of fat
- 38 grams of protein
- 3 grams of net carbs

🕐 **Prep Time: 35 mins | Cook Time: 20 mins**

Ingredients

- 4 boneless chicken thighs
- ¼ cup soy sauce
- 1 fresh jalapeño, minced
- 1 lemon
- 2 cups green beans

Instructions

1. Mix together the minced jalapeño, soy sauce, fresh lemon juice and chicken thighs in a large bowl. Marinate for at least 30 minutes.
2. Fry the marinated chicken thighs in a well-oiled pan on medium heat for 8–10 minutes on each side.
3. Cook green beans in another pan on medium-high heat until slightly browned, about 5–8 minutes.
4. Serve everything together and enjoy!

Lemon Garlic Salmon

Prep time for this dinner is a breeze! Just dress the salmon and steam it and serve on top of zucchini. Velvety soft fish in no time!

Nutrition

495 calories per serving | Makes 2 servings

- 36 grams of fat
- 35 grams of protein
- 3 grams of net carbs

Ingredients

- 2 6-oz. salmon fillets
- 2 cloves garlic
- 4 slices lemon
- 2 tbsp. olive oil
- 1 large zucchini

Instructions

1. On a baking sheet lined with 2 sheets of foil, add olive oil and place 1 salmon fillet onto each sheet of foil. Season with salt and pepper and top with 2 lemon slices each.
2. Slice the garlic and arrange around each salmon. Close each sheet of foil tightly and bake everything at 400°F for 15 minutes.
3. Spiralize the zucchini using a vegetable spiralizer and cook in a lightly oiled pan for no longer than 2 minutes, tossing continuously.
4. Serve the baked salmon on top of a bed of zoodles and enjoy!

Mediterranean Lamb Burger

Greek inspired & seasoned – this variation of a burger will leave you wanting seconds! Best served with creamed spinach.

Nutrition

640 calories per serving | Makes 2 servings

▌	50 grams of fat
▌	38 grams of protein
▌	2 grams of net carbs

🕐 **Prep Time: 5 mins | Cook Time: 15 mins**

Ingredients

- 12 oz. ground lamb
- 1 tbsp. dried rosemary
- 2 oz. goat cheese
- 12 oz. spinach
- ¼ cup sour cream

Instructions

1. Season the lamb with salt, pepper and dried rosemary. Form two, flattened patties and grill or fry until cooked throughout.
2. Cook spinach in an oiled pan until wilted, then add sour cream. Mix well and season with salt and pepper.
3. Add an ounce of goat cheese onto each burger and serve with creamed spinach.

Chicken Zoodle Alfredo

A super creamy and simple dinner that's delightfully delicious! Break out the Parmesan cheese and enjoy liberally in this alfredo recipe!

Nutrition

521 calories per serving | Makes 2 servings

28 grams of fat	
59 grams of protein	
3 grams of net carbs	

🕐 **Prep Time: 5 mins | Cook Time: 20 mins**

Ingredients

- 2 8-oz. chicken breasts
- ¼ cup heavy cream
- ¼ cup Parmesan cheese
- 2 tbsp. unsalted butter
- 200 grams zucchini

Instructions

1. Fry the chicken breasts for about 7 minutes on each side and then slice them into strips.
2. After the chicken is off the pan, lower the flame and melt the butter. Add in heavy cream, Parmesan and cook until thickened.
3. Spiralize the zucchini and pan fry for no longer than 2 minutes.
4. Add the chicken to the zoodles and drizzle with the alfredo sauce.

Baked Dijon Salmon

This is one of our favorite ways to prepare salmon! The Dijon gives it a unique flavor and the pork rind-Parmesan breading gives it a satisfying crunch.

Nutrition

415 calories per serving | Makes 2 servings

25 grams of fat	
40 grams of protein	
2 grams of net carbs	

Ingredients

- 2 6-oz. salmon fillets
- 3 tbsp. Dijon mustard
- 1 oz. pork rinds
- 2 tbsp. Parmesan cheese
- 16 spears asparagus

Instructions

1. Rub the salmon fillets with Dijon mustard on all sides and season with salt and pepper.
2. Pulse the pork rinds and Parmesan cheese until they resemble bread crumbs.
3. Press the salmon firmly into the pork rind-Parmesan breading mixture on all sides.
4. Cut the fibrous ends off the asparagus.
5. Bake the salmon and asparagus on an oiled baking sheet at 400°F for 15 minutes. Enjoy!

Greek Lemon Chicken

Food of the gods! The quick prep and bake time makes dinner easy and delicious. Enjoy olives and spinach as traditional Greek sides.

Nutrition

634 calories per serving | Makes 2 servings

- 54 grams of fat
- 37 grams of protein
- 2 grams of net carbs

🕑 **Prep Time: 35 mins | Cook Time: 30 mins**

Ingredients

- 4 boneless chicken thighs
- ¼ cup olive oil
- 1 lemon
- 4 tbsp. olives
- 4 oz. spinach

Instructions

1. Squeeze the lemon juice into a bowl and add olive oil, salt, pepper and chicken thighs. Marinate for at least 30 minutes, but preferably 4 hours.
2. Bake the marinated chicken thighs at 375°F for 30 minutes.
3. Serve the thighs on a bed of spinach and olives. Add a squeeze of fresh lemon juice.

Creamy Shrimp Scampi

Creamy, saucy shrimp paired with even creamier cauliflower mash makes a great light dinner full of flavor.

Nutrition

660 calories per serving | Makes 2 servings

22 grams of fat

38 grams of protein

3 grams of net carbs

Ingredients

- ½ head cauliflower
- ½ cup heavy cream
- 12 oz. large shrimp, peeled
- 1 tsp. garlic powder
- ½ lemon

Instructions

1. Steam the cauliflower florets for 10 minutes.
2. Blend the florets in a blender with a ¼ cup of heavy cream. Season with salt and pepper.
3. Cook the shrimp on medium heat for 3 minutes on each side or until fully pink. Season with salt and pepper.
4. Add in the rest of the heavy cream, garlic powder and lemon juice. Cook the shrimp for another minute, stirring. Serve and enjoy!

Pepper-Crusted Flank Steak

You'll wonder why you've never broiled a steak before when you try this pepper-crusted flank steak. Crisp and juicy all in one creamy package.

Nutrition

445 calories per serving | Makes 2 servings

27 grams of fat	
38 grams of protein	
5 grams of net carbs	

Ingredients

- 16 spears asparagus
- 12 oz. flank steak
- 6 oz. white or brown mushrooms
- 1 clove garlic
- ¼ cup heavy cream

Instructions

1. Cut the fibrous ends off the asparagus and roast at 400°F for 15 minutes.
2. Liberally season the steak with salt and pepper. Broil for 5 minutes on each side.
3. Cook the mushrooms and a clove of crushed garlic in a well-oiled pan for 8 minutes. Add in heavy cream, stir and allow to thicken.
4. Cover the steak with foil and let it rest for 5 minutes before slicing and serving together.

Ham & Cheddar Quiche

Breakfast for dinner! This hearty, crustless quiche is a great, one-pan dinner that bakes while you set the table!

Nutrition

370 calories per serving | Makes 4 servings

- 30 grams of fat
- 20 grams of protein
- 1.7 grams of net carbs

⏱ **Prep Time: 8 mins | Cook Time: 40 mins**

Ingredients

- 4 large eggs
- ½ cup heavy cream
- 1 cup shredded cheddar cheese
- 1 cup ham, cubed
- 4 stalks green onion

Instructions

1. Crack the eggs into a mixing bowl and whisk with heavy cream until pale yellow.
2. Add in cheddar, ham, chopped green onion and salt and pepper. Stir until well incorporated.
3. Add quiche batter to an oven-safe pan or a cast iron skillet. Bake at 350°F for 40 minutes.
4. Allow to cool lightly then slice and serve.

Shrimp Tartar

Our shrimp tartar dish is delightfully tasty and extremely simple to make. Serve it in a cylindrical shape to impress your guests!

Nutrition

410 calories per serving | Makes 2 servings

- 35 grams of fat
- 35 grams of protein
- 5 grams of net carbs

🕐 **Prep Time: 5 mins | Cook Time: 8 mins**

Ingredients

- 16 oz. large shrimp, peeled
- 1 ½ medium avocados
- 1 campari tomato
- 3 tbsp. mayonnaise
- 1 tsp. Dijon mustard

Instructions

1. Cook the shrimp in a lightly oiled pan on medium heat for about 3 minutes on each side. Add to a mixing bowl with the mayonnaise and Dijon mustard.
2. Dice the avocado and tomato and add them to the bowl as well.
3. Season with salt and pepper to taste and toss everything very well. Serve chilled and enjoy!

Lasagna Express

Lasagna with just 5 ingredients? No way! Yes way. Warning: You may start questioning if lasagna ever had pasta in it in the first place.

Nutrition

573 calories per serving | Makes 4 servings

46 grams of fat	
33 grams of protein	
5 grams of net carbs	

⏱ **Prep Time: 30 mins | Cook Time: 40 mins**

Ingredients

- 1 lb. ground beef
- 1 cup marinara sauce
- 1 large zucchini
- 10 oz. ricotta cheese
- 4 oz. shredded mozzarella

Instructions

1. Preheat oven to 350°F. Peel the zucchini into strips using a vegetable peeler and set aside the cores. Salt the strips and let them sit for 15 minutes. After that, gently squeeze out the excess water using a clean kitchen towel.
2. Brown the ground beef in an oiled frying pan. Add marinara and season well with salt and pepper.
3. Layer into a 9x9" casserole dish: meat, cover with zucchini strips, ricotta, meat, cover with zucchini strips, ricotta, mozzarella.
4. Cover with foil and bake for 30 minutes. Then, broil uncovered for 2–3 minutes to caramelize the top.

Crispy Buffalo Wings

Who knew a classic could be so easy? If you're a fan of spicy, you'll love these simple buffalo wings!

Nutrition

725 calories per serving | Makes 2 servings

- 56 grams of fat
- 49 grams of protein
- 3 grams of net carbs

⏱ **Prep Time: 10 mins | Cook Time: 16 mins**

Ingredients

- 6 chicken wings
- ½ cup *Frank's Red Hot sauce*
- 2 tbsp. unsalted butter
- 6 oz. cole slaw salad mix
- 2 tbsp. mayonnaise

Instructions

1. Separate the chicken wings into 6 wingettes and 6 drumettes. Season with salt and pepper.
2. On a foil-lined baking sheet, broil on high for 16 minutes flipping them all halfway through.
3. Melt *Frank's Red Hot sauce* and the butter in a pan on a very low flame. Season the sauce with salt and pepper.
4. After broiling, toss the wings in the pan with the melted sauce. Serve with a side of the cole slaw salad mixed with mayonnaise.

Tip: *Cole slaw is best served cold so make it ahead of time and chill it in the refrigerator.*

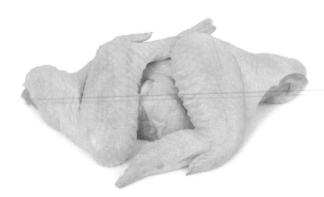

Hollandaise Salmon

Zesty and creamy! Hollandaise sauce pairs perfectly with the flavor and texture of salmon. Easier to make than you think!

Nutrition

415 calories per serving | Makes 2 servings

- 28 grams of fat
- 37 grams of protein
- 3 grams of net carbs

Ingredients

- 2 6-oz. salmon fillets
- 1 large egg yolk
- 1 tbsp. lemon juice
- 2 tbsp. unsalted butter, cubed
- 1 large zucchini

Instructions

1. Pan fry the salmon fillets for 5 minutes on each side. Set them aside after cooking.
2. Whisk the egg yolk in a double boiler until pale yellow. Add lemon juice and whisk until thickened.
3. Add a tablespoon of butter at a time until each is incorporated into the sauce. Add a teaspoon of water if the sauce becomes too thick.
4. Spiralize the zucchini into zoodles using a vegetable spiralizer. Fry the zoodles in a lightly oiled pan for no longer than 2 minutes, tossing continuously.
5. Serve everything together and enjoy!

Thyme Butter Basted Ribeye

Crispy on the outside, juicy on the inside and basted with thyme and butter — a classic low-carb dinner that'll impress and satisfy.

Nutrition

745 calories per serving | Makes 2 servings

- 65 grams of fat
- 32 grams of protein
- 5 grams of net carbs

Ingredients

- 12 oz. ribeye steak
- 2 tbsp. unsalted butter
- 2 sprigs fresh thyme
- 6 oz. Brussels sprouts
- 2 tbsp. olive oil

Instructions

1. Salt the steak liberally for 4 hours before cooking and keep in the refrigerator.
2. Toss the Brussels sprouts in olive oil and roast them for 25 minutes at 375°F.
3. Heat up an oiled skillet until very hot. Cook the steak for 4 minutes on first side (this will make a medium rare steak).
4. Flip, add butter and thyme, and baste with a spoon for another 4 minutes while frying.
5. Let the steak rest, covered, for 5 minutes and enjoy with the roasted Brussels sprouts.

Cheesy Portobello Burgers

Mushroom lovers rejoice! These Portobello burgers are a twist on traditional burgers and stuffed mushrooms and will leave you craving more!

Nutrition

675 calories per serving | Makes 2 servings

	49 grams of fat
	52 grams of protein
	4 grams of net carbs

Ingredients

- 2 portobello mushrooms
- 12 oz. ground beef
- 4 oz. shredded cheddar cheese
- 1 oz. baby spinach
- 4 tbsp. Parmesan cheese

Instructions

1. Mince the mushroom stems and spinach and combine with beef, cheddar, salt & pepper.
2. Make two patties and press into the underside of the mushrooms.
3. Bake on a baking sheet at 375°F for 10 minutes. Sprinkle Parmesan on top & bake for 5 more minutes.

Optional: *Broil for 2 minutes to caramelize the Parmesan.*

Thank You

Our hopes are that some of these dinners will become staples in your diet making low-carb cooking more delicious and easier for you on a daily basis.

If you have questions, suggestions or any other feedback, please don't hesitate to contact us directly: hello@tasteaholics.com.

We answer emails every day and we'd love to hear from you. Each comment we receive is valuable and helps us in continuing to provide quality content.

Your direct feedback could be used to help others discover the benefits of going low-carb!

If you have a success story, please send it to us! We're always happy to hear about our readers' success.

Thank you again and we hope you have enjoyed *Dinner in Five*!

— *Vicky Ushakova & Rami Abramov*

About the Authors

Vicky Ushakova and Rami Abramov co-founded Tasteaholics.com to provide an easy way to understand why the ketogenic diet is truly effective for weight loss and health management. They create recipes that are low-carb, high-fat and maximize flavor. The books in their *Keto in Five* series are wildly popular among the low-carb community due to their simplicity and efficacy.

Vicky and Rami's mission is to continue to improve their audience's health and outlook on life through diet and nutrition education. They are dedicated to helping change the detrimental nutritional guidelines in the United States and across the globe that have been plaguing millions of people over the last 40 years.

The duo travels the world to explore new cultures, cuisines and culinary techniques which they pass on through new recipes and content available on their website.

Personal Notes

Use these pages to write down any recipe notes and more delicious ideas.

References

1. Aude, Y., A. S, Agatston, F. Lopez-Jimenez, et al. "The National Cholesterol Education Program Diet vs a Diet Lower in Carbohydrates and Higher in Protein and Monounsaturated Fat: A Randomized Trial." JAMA Internal Medicine 164, no. 19 (2004): 2141–46. doi: 10.1001/archinte.164.19.2141. jamanetwork.com/journals/jamainternalmedicine/article-abstract/217514.

2. De Lau, L. M., M. Bornebroek, J. C. Witteman, A. Hofman, P. J. Koudstaal, and M. M. Breteler. "Dietary Fatty Acids and the Risk of Parkinson Disease: The Rotterdam Study." Neurology 64, no. 12 (June 2005): 2040–5. doi:10.1212/01.WNL.0000166038.67153.9F. www.ncbi.nlm.nih.gov/pubmed/15985568/.

3. Freeman, J. M., E. P. Vining, D. J. Pillas, P. L. Pyzik, J. C. Casey, and L M. Kelly. "The Efficacy of the Ketogenic Diet-1998: A Prospective Evaluation of Intervention in 150 Children." Pediatrics 102, no. 6 (December 1998): 1358–63. www.ncbi.nlm.nih.gov/pubmed/9832569/.

4. Hemingway, C, J. M. Freeman, D. J. Pillas, and P. L. Pyzik. "The Ketogenic Diet: A 3- to 6-Year Follow-up of 150 Children Enrolled Prospectively. Pediatrics 108, no. 4 (October 2001): 898–905. www.ncbi.nlm.nih.gov/pubmed/11581442/.

5. Henderson, S. T. "High Carbohydrate Diets and Alzheimer's Disease." Medical Hypotheses 62, no. 5 (2014): 689–700. doi:10.1016/j.mehy.2003.11.028. www.ncbi.nlm.nih.gov/pubmed/15082091/.

6. Neal, E.G., H. Chaffe, R. H. Schwartz, M. S. Lawson, N. Edwards, G. Fitzsimmons, A. Whitney, and J. H. Cross. "The Ketogenic Diet for the Treatment of Childhood Epilepsy: A Randomised Controlled Trial." Lancet Neurology 7, no. 6 (June 2008): 500–506. doi:10.1016/S1474-4422(08)70092-9. www.ncbi.nlm.nih.gov/pubmed/18456557.

7. Chowdhury, R., S. Warnakula, S. Kunutsor, F. Crowe, H. A. Ward, L. Johnson, et al. "Association of Dietary, Circulating, and Supplement Fatty Acids with Coronary Risk: A Systematic Review and Meta-Analysis." Annals of Internal Medicine 160 (2014): 398–406. doi:10.7326/M13-1788. annals.org/article.aspx?articleid=1846638.

8. Siri-Tarino, P. W., Q. Sun, F. B. Hu, and R. M. Krauss. "Meta-Analysis of Prospective Cohort Studies Evaluating the Association of Saturated Fat with Cardiovascular Disease." American Journal of Clinical Nutrition 91, no. 3 (March 2010): 535–46. doi:10.3945/ajcn.2009.27725. www.ncbi.nlm.nih.gov/pubmed/20071648.

9. "Prediabetes and Insulin Resistance," The National Institute of Diabetes and Digestive and Kidney Diseases. https://www.niddk.nih.gov/health-information/diabetes/types/prediabetes-insulin-resistance.

10. "National Diabetes Statistics Report," Centers for Disease Control and Prevention, 2014. http://www.cdc.gov/diabetes/pubs/statsreport14/national-diabetes-report-web.pdf.

11. Dyson, P. A., Beatty, S. and Matthews, D. R. "A low-carbohydrate diet is more effective in reducing body weight than healthy eating in both diabetic and non-diabetic subjects." Diabetic Medicine. 2007. 24: 1430–1435. http://onlinelibrary.wiley.com/doi/10.1111/j.1464-5491.2007.02290.x/full.

12. Christopher D. Gardner, PhD; Alexandre Kiazand, MD; Sofiya Alhassan, PhD; Soowon Kim, PhD; Randall S. Stafford, MD, PhD; Raymond R. Balise, PhD; Helena C. Kraemer, PhD; Abby C. King, PhD, "Comparison of the Atkins, Zone, Ornish, and LEARN Diets for Change in Weight and Related Risk Factors Among Overweight Premenopausal Women," JAMA. 2007;297(9):969-977. http://jama.jamanetwork.com/article.aspx?articleid=205916.

13. Gary D. Foster, Ph.D., Holly R. Wyatt, M.D., James O. Hill, Ph.D., Brian G. McGuckin, Ed.M., Carrie Brill, B.S., B. Selma Mohammed, M.D., Ph.D., Philippe O. Szapary, M.D., Daniel J. Rader, M.D., Joel S. Edman, D.Sc., and Samuel Klein, M.D., "A Randomized Trial of a Low-Carbohydrate Diet for Obesity – NEJM," N Engl J Med 2003; 348:2082-2090. http://www.nejm.org/doi/full/10.1056/NEJMoa022207.

14. JS Volek, MJ Sharman, AL Gómez, DA Judelson, MR Rubin, G Watson, B Sokmen, R Silvestre, DN French, and WJ Kraemer, "Comparison of Energy-restricted Very Low-carbohydrate and Low-fat Diets on Weight Loss and Body Composition in Overweight Men and Women," Nutr Metab (Lond). 2004; 1: 13. http://www.ncbi.nlm.nih.gov/pmc/articles/PMC538279/.

15. Y. Wady Aude, MD; Arthur S. Agatston, MD; Francisco Lopez-Jimenez, MD, MSc; Eric H. Lieberman, MD; Marie Almon, MS, RD; Melinda Hansen, ARNP; Gerardo Rojas, MD; Gervasio A. Lamas, MD; Charles H. Hennekens, MD, DrPH, "The National Cholesterol Education Program Diet vs a Diet Lower in Carbohydrates and Higher in Protein and Monounsaturated Fat," Arch Intern Med. 2004;164(19):2141-2146. http://archinte.jamanetwork.com/article.aspx?articleid=217514.

16. Bonnie J. Brehm, Randy J. Seeley, Stephen R. Daniels, and David A. D'Alessio, "A Randomized Trial Comparing a Very Low Carbohydrate Diet and a Calorie-Restricted Low Fat Diet on Body Weight and Cardiovascular Risk Factors in Healthy Women," The Journal of Clinical Endocrinology & Metabolism: Vol 88, No 4; January 14, 2009. http://press.endocrine.org/doi/full/10.1210/jc.2002-021480.

17. M. E. Daly, R. Paisey, R. Paisey, B. A. Millward, C. Eccles, K. Williams, S. Hammersley, K. M. MacLeod, T. J. Gale, "Short-term Effects of Severe Dietary Carbohydrate-restriction Advice in Type 2 Diabetes–a Randomized Controlled Trial," Diabetic Medicine, 2006; 23: 15–20. http://onlinelibrary.wiley.com/doi/10.1111/j.1464-5491.2005.01760.x/abstract.

18. Stephen B. Sondike, MD, Nancy Copperman, MS, RD, Marc S. Jacobson, MD, "Effects Of A Low-Carbohydrate Diet On Weight Loss And Cardiovascular Risk Factor In Overweight Adolescents," The Journal of Pediatrics: Vol 142, Issue 3: 253-258; March 2003. http://www.sciencedirect.com/science/article/pii/S0022347602402065.

19. William S. Yancy Jr., MD, MHS; Maren K. Olsen, PhD; John R. Guyton, MD; Ronna P. Bakst, RD; and Eric C. Westman, MD, MHS, "A Low-Carbohydrate, Ketogenic Diet versus a Low-Fat Diet To Treat Obesity and Hyperlipidemia: A Randomized, Controlled Trial," Ann Intern Med. 2004;140(10):769-777. http://annals.org/article.aspx?articleid=717451.

20. Grant D Brinkworth, Manny Noakes, Jonathan D Buckley, Jennifer B Keogh, and Peter M Clifton, "Long-term Effects of a Very-low-carbohydrate Weight Loss Diet Compared with an Isocaloric Low-fat Diet after 12 Mo," Am J Clin Nutr July 2009 vol. 90 no. 1 23-32. http://ajcn.nutrition.org/content/90/1/23.long.

21. H. Guldbrand, B. Dizdar, B. Bunjaku, T. Lindström, M. Bachrach-Lindström, M. Fredrikson, C. J. Östgren, F. H. Nystrom, "In Type 2 Diabetes, Randomisation to Advice to Follow a Low-carbohydrate Diet Transiently Improves Glycaemic Control Compared with Advice to Follow a Low-fat Diet Producing a Similar Weight Loss," Diabetologia (2012) 55: 2118. http://link.springer.com/article/10.1007/s00125-012-2567-4.

22. Sharon M. Nickols-Richardson, PhD, RD, , Mary Dean Coleman, PhD, RD, Joanne J. Volpe, Kathy W. Hosig, PhD, MPH, RD, "Perceived Hunger Is Lower and Weight Loss Is Greater in Overweight Premenopausal Women Consuming a Low-Carbohydrate/High-Protein vs High-Carbohydrate/Low-Fat Diet," The Journal of Pediatrics: Vol 105, Issue 9: 1433–1437; September 2005. http://www.sciencedirect.com/science/article/pii/S000282230501151X.

23. Frederick F. Samaha, M.D., Nayyar Iqbal, M.D., Prakash Seshadri, M.D., Kathryn L. Chicano, C.R.N.P., Denise A. Daily, R.D., Joyce McGrory, C.R.N.P., Terrence Williams, B.S., Monica Williams, B.S., Edward J. Gracely, Ph.D., and Linda Stern, M.D., "A Low-Carbohydrate as Compared with a Low-Fat Diet in Severe Obesity, " N Engl J Med 2003; 348:2074-2081. http://www.nejm.org/doi/full/10.1056/NEJMoa022637.

24. Yancy WS Jr, Westman EC, McDuffie JR, Grambow SC, Jeffreys AS, Bolton J, Chalecki A, Oddone EZ, "A randomized trial of a low-carbohydrate diet vs orlistat plus a low-fat diet for weight loss," Arch Intern Med. 2010 Jan 25;170(2):136-45. http://www.ncbi.nlm.nih.gov/pubmed/20101008?itool=EntrezSystem2.PEntrez.Pubmed.Pubmed_ResultsPanel.Pubmed_RVDocSum&ordinalpos=2.

25. Swasti Tiwari, Shahla Riazi, and Carolyn A. Ecelbarger, "Insulin's Impact on Renal Sodium Transport and Blood Pressure in Health, Obesity, and Diabetes," American Journal of Physiology vol. 293, no. 4 (October 2, 2007): 974–984, http://ajprenal.physiology.org/content/293/4/F974.full.

30895582R00056

Printed in Great
Britain
by Amazon